D1487358

God's Bicycle

Joel Peckham

FUTURECYCLE PRESS

www.futurecycle.org

Library of Congress Control Number: 2015931262

Published by FutureCycle Press
Lexington, Kentucky, USA

ISBN 978-1-938853-61-6

For the Students and Faculty of UC-Clermont College

Contents

Everything Must Go

Making Contact

Acknowledgments

Everything Must Go

Psalm 96

Sing to the Lord a new song—of men and women riding
the last bus home through quarries and yellowing
tobacco fields of Highway 421. Sing the long sigh
and slow grind of axels and tired eyes that watch
through glass the memory of Guthrie and Bluff Hills
and the Greenback Labor Party that never had a chance to
sing of strong arms and backs that broke in heat and boys
and girls who'd grow barefoot through stones and stagnant
water and bellies swole with hunger. Sing malaria, pellagra,
and the scars that faded and the scars that didn't. Sing
a new song from the old, the way things work their way
like hookworm up and in through cracks in the skin. Sing
their descendants up from the dust to work in Michigan
auto plants and down to dust again in mines of West Virginia.
Sing cornbread and potatoes. Sing food stamps and long lines
and the water shut-off notice on the door. Sing thirst and stink
and the boys signed up to fight through mustard gas and jungle,
the beaches of Europe and the Philippines, the deserts
of the Middle East. Sing of IEDs and what freedom really means
to empty bellies and an anger at everything. Sing of sand—
how it gets everywhere—hair, the pits of your arms, groin,
grinding away the skin like hunger gets everywhere. How
sometimes the only thing to put in an empty hand is another
hand. Sing anger and lust and football on cold Friday nights—
the crush of bodies on bodies. Sing full-contact and sex
in muscle cars on back country roads and in the basements
and parking lots. Sing of children and more children, the 99-cent
burgers and cold fries, the grease that fills them. Sing the grease
that makes the stomach clamp. And single mothers who learned
from their mothers whose men were gone before they were gone,
even when they were there. Sing cosmetology school, beauty
school, and the community college down the road. Because
you're 50 years old and still trying, still singing—man gone.
Kids trying to be gone and you stealing hours on the nursing home
computer where you work wiping asses and cleaning bedpans

so you can take a night class on Gender issues, so you can learn
words like "patriarchy," "hegemony," "abject," "subaltern." Sing
the privilege you're supposed to have. Sing the spirit. Sing
to the Lord, because the Lord is hope that maybe a new song
can rise green and leafy from a bitter soil. Sing, because it's all
you have—this life bound up in other lives before you
that matter because you say they do, you say you do
because you sing.

Movers and Shakers

Lord, let me shake / With purpose
—James Dickey, "The Strength of Fields"

Listen, you can hear them—dragging the past
on blankets over smooth wood floors, loading bureaus
on dollies. Clicking, creaking, grunting with effort,
a man descends the stair, eyes forward, chin high, hair
matted with sweat and sighs, a hundred-year-old
hutch strapped to his back. A subtle quiver
in the calves, a tremble in the neck. In the truck
a driver checks and rechecks the list, figures
weight and cost. They always underestimate
and not by a little. Yes, this will cost
a hell of a lot. But who can really figure the way
a life accumulates until it is boxed, stacked,
packed to fill the yard, the truck

　　　　　—that's twice as much
as you quoted! Yassir but your weight was off
at least a thousand pounds. We figure
by weight—your piano alone....

　　　　　He has learned to take
their anger the way a fisherman takes weather, a fact
of life, impersonal to him. Anger never is about
the cause. And, after all, they have to pay or leave
the marriage bed, the crib, stereo, boxes
of clothes and toys—to sit, overnight or longer
in the drive. Their lives left open to wind
and rain, the inspection of neighbors—
a judgment worse than God's. Moving is hard
enough. To move is to risk—and for what,
to where? So many things piled and poorly
placed. Always on the verge of tipping, shattering
in the dark, the whole living world trembling around.

Husks

1.

A Chevy up on blocks is only an eyesore
to the faithless.

2.

—Keeper of exhaled breath, watcher
of what was, arc of stutter, shudder
and cough, chamber of wants, of
spent muscle in the thighs
and backs and jaws—
                              When all
that's left is shell and rust, what waits
to be reborn? This old
muscular husk churns—
rusted country roads and half-
abandoned parking lots.
I could spend a life pointing
at miracles of light that pass
though spiders-silk of shattered
windshields. Nothing aches so like
the broken spine of a drive-shaft,
nothing yearns like an engine almost
turning over in the pre-dawn light.

Blind Spots

Enclosed in glass, in freon, in the soft low purr
of air, a boy drifts in and out of sleep, aware
and unaware that he's been staring for hours
as children on the edge of 80 toss meat-scraps

to strays that yap and paw or growl—
dance in, dance off—one dog nips
the heel of a girl whose legs outgrow
her little dress over and over as the car creeps

forward. Someday the boy will remember it as
sexual, romantic, a continual and unending flash
of white at the hem of an outgrown skirt—
the slash of dirt that seemed to travel up

a thigh forever calling like a road suddenly
open beyond all accidents over and over
in the quick-step and clatter of heels
on asphalt or a long predatory look

of hunger. Boxes of food spill and scatter—
freeze-dried, fast-frozen, microwavable,
precooked—their scents sealed off
from weary drivers who sit and

wonder at a breeze blown strong enough to tip
a twenty-ton truck into their path
and wonder where that wind is going—has
gone—having no suitable frame for a thing that

moves each time you grasp it and moves on.

Traffic

You are now entering Kansas
Or another state just like it —Bumper sticker

They're out there. Cursing, pleading with the radio,
watches flashing with sun. Stagnant pools form
between the shoulders beneath a business suit—a hundred,
a thousand business suits, pantsuits, working casuals.
At the temples a vein begins to swell. In Pennsylvania
a bridge shudders under the weight of waiting cargo:
boxes of food frozen in dry ice, arteries blooming
with soot and smoke and the accumulated heat
of prayer: *Please God, I have a meeting, a wedding*

a ballgame, a doctor's appointment and the needle
pushes into red toward empty. Or hot. Necks strain
to find a gap the eyes can pass through. Someone
stares at a map, mumbling names of roads: 128, 80,
75, Route 2, 31, 15. They are all impassable,
impossible as the long passage of corn rows shook
with summer wind. In the breakdown lane, bent
under the hood, someone is waving his hands at steam

as if warding off imaginary wasps, ghosts, the broken
lines that stretch through tunnels and off-ramps, high
over rivers and other roads and deep into the sides
of mountains. In darkness a small boy wonders
what kinds of tools it took, what kinds of people
to head into a wall of earth and come out again—
earth-fired, beaming—wonders if he can or will. In Ohio
a woman tastes iron in the air, rolls up the window.
For there are signs—there always are—some green, some

white. Shaking with shaken roads and words submerged
in haze that on a clear night with the road open would
emerge like prophecy: 20 MILES TO THE GREAT

DIVIDE. 30 MILES TO NIAGARA FALLS. 240 MILES TO
DISNEY WORLD. IDAHO WELCOMES YOU. AMERICA
BEGINS HERE in Paris, Maine (pop.134), Geneva,
Texas, or Monticello, Arkansas. They are here,
they are coming, stalled and running, from Leechfield
to Holland, Bucksnort to Bulls Gap to Leavenworth where

the Suburban on 35 has been entering Kansas
for hours and the Subaru traveling north may never leave
Illinois. Even the cab driver on the Garden State has gone
silent, gone hoarse—sick of traffic reports and alternate routes
he doubts anyone has been to. They aren't telling. Aren't coming
back. And even if you got out of the car, hopped the median, scaled
the soundproof barrier to the well-manicured lawns of Saddle River
or Newton, what then? Who would be there for you? Better to wait
with the sound off, think of a girl you knew in high school, sitting
by some other sign on some other road, her daughter pleading to go
to the bathroom. Or think of other roads that must lead somewhere

after all, with so many on them on the way
to someplace or another
just like it.

U-Haul: On Highway 65 North of Louisville, Kentucky

The back end of the U-Haul tries to shake
its caging free from the ache of hands,
a steering column shook with heavy rain.
The lock is loose and steel slams steel
as a bed frame winks and jostles under years
of toys they couldn't bear to leave
behind or give away or toss clanging into the iron
dumpster that bloomed beyond belief, beyond
proportion with their little house, little lives
and plans, and still there is so much—these years
of trunks and clothes that don't fit anyone packed,
stacked and roped to walls, taking on the hope
of diets and medications and promise green
as grass in another place, another town where
the divan, a bicycle with a broken chain, box springs,
the pull-out sofa could come to rest again
and live

        (how is it the new start always begins
in the past, going back so far that we keep even
what could break us when what could break us
is so little)

        somewhere north of Louisville and south
of here—that strange sense it is all too much after all,
that we left something important back there and it is gone
and not gone, shuddering high above and behind and far out
in front of us.

Closed to Thru-Traffic

Outside, a scraping, a grating; dust
rises in the heat and, long before dusk,
dusk settles on narrow streets. Workers
move slow, sweat gray. Faces,
hands, hair, lungs streaked ashen
with another day, another paycheck,
eight more hours, 92 degrees and a road
torn up and rising like a dry mist in wet
heat. The mother of the medical student
on the corner lot looks up and swears
as the ultra-pure white siding dims
like a lantern in fog

           Damn-it   I
just power washed those walls

                    pulls out
her cell, slams the door of her car. Tires spin
a fine spray at the knees of the man
with the yellow vest who seems to smile
a little when drivers ease their windows
down enough to shout *I live here* and pull
around angrily before he waves them on.
Years ago, he might have worked the steel
mill by the river, or maybe he's the bastard
son of the son of the barons who ran
this town. Now the steel is gone and he
moves slow if he moves at all, listens
to the flats of shovels throw sparks
on uneven ground and, whatever he thinks,

he thinks to himself, solid, steady as any
stone outcropping wearing away the ocean
and sending it back upon itself.

Everything Must Go

In the parking lot, behind the Dollar General, at two
in the afternoon, a young man thrusts hands
into pockets of an old three-button suit fit
for someone half his size—as if he might
have fished it from a thrift store or a pile
of clothes at a yard sale, estate sale, auction
for the peeling home behind the elementary
school where people pick and peck at tables
on the outgrown lawn, silent as hungry

blackbirds after grubs. Nobody looks
into windows, knocks on doors. Nothing
to see here. Nothing they haven't seen before
on every street in town. Another sign goes
up. Another. And someone gets a tax break
when he buys the place on Market for half
of what it's worth. *And, damn, if they'd a let us
pay that price to start, we could a kept
the bastard. Or if the Ford plant didn't move or if—*

And the walls ache empty as the stomachs
of strays who wade sun-splashed in river water
with a girl off Route 222. Everything idles.
Engines, low on gas, turn over, sputter out a grinding
song. Everything's for sale. For rent. Fore-
closed. *Everything must go.* And the young man

hums a melody that could be a spiritual, though
he doesn't look like a boy to sing spirituals. Too
mod, too hip, too fashionably poor. And no one
sings those old songs anymore, having lost the feel,
the touch that looks you up and down and says *I know,*
because we do. Or should. After all, it's nothing

we haven't heard before: the way we mutter
to ourselves, taking as we do what falls
to us with hands open as any supplicant's. How
many doors swing idly in and out? And, tell me, who
wore the jackets we are wearing now?

In the Next Seat

At the Greyhound Station, Nashville, Tennessee

A man sits in stink. The little girl
asleep against his chest has wet
them both from Atlanta through
Chattanooga and he's
as scared to wake her
as you might be to wake
the dead. Awake could be
anything, could be vomit or
weeping or the non-stop
chatter of the wired. And how
we would all wish for sleep now—
how a stink in dreams can seem
to break things down, mingle
salt, piss, deodorant gasoline,

distance. Too much
distance. A little girl sleeping
on a man's lap in Middle
Tennessee can be
a thousand things, all of them
having everything and nothing
to do with the woman
in the second row who keeps
wanting to know why we need
to stop at every piece-of-shit
podunk nothing town from here
to Alaska or the man who says,
dead serious, *this bus don't go*
there, only to Gary, you'll
have to catch another
or how I need to go

to the bathroom and don't know
if I can climb the seat in front

of me without hitting some sleeping
arm or leg with a knee, a stray
foot. So I think of how John Glenn,
pissing in his spacesuit, swore
he saw something bright and alive
through window of his capsule,
fireflies, livings sparks, wheeling,
dancing in the void. How it was
only dust, backlit and shining

with a million stars. So, sealed off
or in, we wish for any kind of contact
and fear it. Coming over the hills
of Chattanooga, looking for shadows
in the wood, or into moonroofs,
into windshields, into the eyes of neon
signs where Sam is always sad and Charlie
nervous, and fireworks can be had
for a couple of dollars a dozen
with boiled peanuts and diesel fuel.

But the sparks are only headlights
gliding on a mirrored surface
and our own eyes staring back,
heavy and lurching as any bus
that never seems to want
to get going again, in no
particular hurry to let the air
rush in and leave this place
because it carries everything
along: the man beside me,
the little girl, the stink
of any life that breathes
just near you but is not
yours, could never be, like any
answer or any distant dream
of sleep.

Pollack, 51

Stop the Car. Let me out!
—Edith Metzger

These are not windows or boxes are not rooms and if you fool yourself that
you can see into them through them well watch yourself—that's on you—
the way you see that painting Pollack poured upon the glass so paint
becomes a thing that stops you on your way to him—a fired burst of red or
soldered blue a darkening convergence he saw then stepped into with you
—this before he lost himself in alcohol again before the crash that splashed
his skull against a tree and sent two women flying from the car—of course
he did for when he wasn't crashing he was always on the edge of going off
and you can shout for him to stop and let you out but he forgot that you
were there long before he started which is to say that he forgot himself and
he like you like glass was just a vessel for the color and the light and for its
absence in the way you might experience a waterfall a wall of water
coming down from great heights falling heaving fast and cold as you stand
near enough to feel its sting upon the canvas of your skin to see the way the
light moves shatters and reflects its frothing which is the one becoming
many like a chain of people holding hands as they are pulled apart by
gravity and into space that reaches back while moving forward at the same
time to the same place as we must before we scatter into atoms or maybe
you are drawn to stand beneath its force and upward at its face or pass
through not to see the mountainside but feel the charge the force of
passage and survive to look back from the other side still cold and shivering
wet with marvels at the shining there which is just light caught shifting on
a waterfall like so many words we use to try to pull us close to what we are
have been—words—like "canvas" and "splash" or "vessels" tossed upon
these roaring surfaces that only seem as still and silent as a pane of glass.

O Street

Lincoln, Nebraska

You have heard the rumor this street ends somewhere past the railroad tracks, petering out with the last of the asphalt before a river, or a cornfield, or in a distant city at the edge of Iowa. Don't believe it. How can nothing pass into nothing without continuation? This is a street where no one lives but everyone works, where every breath is wind-blown and like paper driven past the stoplights over the rise in the hill to the blackened windows of a "gentlemen's club" where a neon woman, her mouth open, whispers her lie—*we want you here, anything can be bought*. Streets like this go on, endless in the urban sprawl of every dying city in America. So I will speak of it as a kind of prayer for the empty house on the corner of 27th with the sloping porch and for-sale sign hanging loose on the door, everyone knowing it will not be sold or occupied, knowing that my words with nothing left to stop them will reach beyond the Wyuka Place of Rest— est. 1869, beyond the Forbidden City oriental restaurant, the Texaco, Robbins Mortuary, past the Gateway Mall, beyond this town, down the river, through cornrows, to reach another road, Highway 80 or 35, and pick up speed all the way through Pennsylvania, to New York, to the Atlantic, and then straight to the ears of God—a prayer of continuation, of existence, traveling the corridors of the throat saying *O* and again *O* and *O, O, O*.

Peace and the Valley

Everything recedes as we rise, through Cumberland
and Cheat River. I crane my neck toward the crest,
chest to the wheel—a body strung tight like fence-wire,
like fear. The world is only what I can see—and I
can't see far—beyond this little car this glowing space
I carry with me and around me but is not mine. Anything
could enter; snow churns against the windshield
as my son shifts fitfully in sleep, curled around himself,
caught in the current of a dream. On the radio, Elvis,
singing about peace in the valley, and I think of him
at 22, bent over a piano, reaching for himself through
all those voices that he learned to emulate by listening
outside the echo chamber of a church or on a storefront
porch where worn brown hands slapped down straight
rhythm, and it's in there deep in all the voices
of the Jordanaires—layering around him, pushing in
and pulling back, sidling on up close like drunken friends
come home along the same path saying *Brother,*
let's lean on each other for a while, just until we get
our feet—and when they do, it's gospel. His voice
is warm and sure and young and ancient like the song,
already older than it had a right to be when Dorsey
penned it for Mahalia—this kid entering a space
like it was made for him—and he makes himself a home
there and a faith no one could question. For a moment

I am thinking of the valley in the distance and a farm
with windows flamed by firelight, surrounded by the night
and this snow, this killing snow, and how it must seem
peaceful there, falling heavy, piling up around that space,
those people who are not headed anywhere but where
they are, and yet, like all of us, hurtling through
a blizzard of stars. And I want to feel the earth beneath me,
but it moves. No. I move and slip, gain traction again.

And there is only what I cannot see: the road ahead,
the mountain's crest, taillights buoyed in a night
that's passed to weightlessness. Somewhere below,
a river rushes fast and freezing, deceptively dark
and deep from Shavers Fork and Blackfork upward
through Albright to the Monongahela, the Ohio,
Mississippi and the Gulf. I long for its reach,
its steady progress, its being everywhere
and so many and—always—free.

You Tell Me All My Love Poems Are About Myself

They are. Of course they are. The way a stomach
clenches on itself, hungry as a half-starved wolf, and burns.
When I am miles from home and low on cash and the gas-
tank swallows fuel at almost four bucks a gallon, I swallow
down the miles, listening to Gram and Emmy Lou,
and even the light tastes like wind in an empty bowl.
All along Route 52, the train chases evening into the haze
of field-smoke, and it is steel and iron and bitter. I want
you. I want you. I want to breathe you in and sweat you

out like fever. If I said I see the curving of your back,
your taut skin, stretch of stomach and breast rising
with grasses blown down by passing trucks or trains
that raise again to back roads and the swaying hips
of hills, would you still say *This*
is about you like everything longed for is about
the one who wants? But say that every crop
in wind sings back your name. Say the farmhouse
leaning into itself from years of rot and rain calls back

the story of your father when he took a rifle to the barns
to shoot a hog. *He had to,* you said. *She was sick.*
But that wasn't the point. It never is. The things
we have to do we have to pay for. I imagine him
walking across the yard, throwing the gun into the truck,
swinging himself up and in. *She understands,*
he thinks—and hates himself. And so it is

about him too. And every stoplight in the city
of Portsmouth. Every other car that can't move
fast enough through roadwork merging lanes
and intersections. It is about love, which is always
about the wanting. That space between Adam's fingers
and the hand of God that might as well be 190 miles
of road. Is more. Is all the roads that bend through
mountains. And how like water lovers seek the hollows

and the shallows. How your mouth fills my mouth,
your breast the empty cup of my hand. How bodies fit
and fill and form to one another over time. But not
just that—the way an image fills the mind, the chest

and lungs: you curled in sleep at five a.m. You reading
to our boy at night, his arm across your chest. You
at fourteen painting a fence on your father's farm—white
smear on a calf that rises up and into cut-off jeans. You
at seven spinning and dancing until, delirious, you fall
against the hearth. The quarter-moon of scar it left
by your right eye that pulls me now through fields
and hills, grunting and sniffing at the air—a thirst,
a hunger worth starving for. This specific, holy
wanting that is you.

Making Contact

The Basement Man

How lucky do you think you are,
he asks, his weathered hand slipping
past a new bulge in the wall, a crack
just wide enough to fit a clotted fingernail.
It rained for days until the clay
that holds up mountains shifted,
a drainpipe cracked,
the all-dry system split a seam;
or maybe it was just too much
water, too much earth, too
much pressure pushing in from all
directions, until something
gave. Not everything. Not yet. And so
the basement man takes measurements.
I could sink a sump down there. That will
get the overflow. Drill a hole through
here. But the wall.... And I'm thinking
money, thinking time and men who place
a hand against a pipe, a stone, a spine
and feel it fissure. What would it mean
to place my hands to walls and roads
and on the backs of men
and women and feel foundations
shift? Like most, I've waited: lights
off, head down. I've pulled open
the wooden cellar doors in winter, run
my hand along the canning jars
and smelled that dank air of things stacked
and packed against the cold and time
and loss, knowing walls cave and
basements crumble—but not how
or when. I've learned not to hear,
not to see, not to feel the midnight creak
and buckle of all things. And I've told
myself I'm luckier than this.

Living in Layers

Mesazoic Gallery, Morrill Hall, University of Nebraska
—*for Cyrus Atefat-Peckham 1998-2004*

A shout, and mammoths shudder.
Bones which once frightened you
to desperate weeping seem
to quiver as you run, back and across
and forward again, like some sun-blown
shell on white sandstone. That light
and blinding. Son, we are walking
again through ages, me reverent, solemn,
you skipping, dancing in and out
of the ropes which cordon off
the dead from the dead from the living.

—*Jurassic, Paleolithic, Mesozoic*—

                                        and you

stop—in the gallery of the great inland
waterway where walls shudder
with an ancient sea—the artist
stopping jaws in hunger on the spines
of sharks, eyes (so many eyes) glassed in
with something like longing. But this
does not matter to a boy lost in some

strange cold thrill on a Midwest Saturday
morning in July; what matters is the stone
beneath your feet, beneath the plexiglass
partition where bones of a great bulldog
tarpon swim eternally northward,
block-jawed and dangerous. You jump

back and scream in fear,

                no,

                    delight, then
stomp and stomp and stomp on the glass
as if to shake the fish, the walls, the sea itself

to life with all its ages and no one to stop you.

Infield/Outfield

Soft sounds. Wind sweeps the lake, the grass.
A gate swings on an old hinge; muffled chatter:
Hey batter batter hey old man hey batter batter.
Hit one here. He thinks, *So it's like this at last,*
everything around him fading, failing—the light,
his eyes. Sometimes a memory, a muscle grips tight
in his back, his chest. But here on the field, time
itself seems tame, indolent, and nothing's lost—
perhaps less waggle in the stroke, the hips, everything
honed down to what is absolute. His hands still sing
in the wood, at the shock of contact. Far out, the last
boy waves and laughs, stumbling to the warning track,
but this one's gone; this one won't be coming back.

Coaching the Swing

nothing comes from nothing —Shakespeare
never start from zero —Joel Peckham, Sr.

1.

Each word is far too much and not enough
because he's seen the perfect swing enough
to see it doesn't matter. That pure stroke is
only wood through air unless it's felt. An eel
in water ten feet down, light made flesh, made
earth again, the way that every grain
of dirt can hum along the legs. And silence is
the muted sound of everything alive. Place
your hand onto the barrel of a gun and you can feel
the bullet that has passed and soon might pass again.
Run your fingertips along a woman's skin and
you will sense ten generations on. That sweet space
in wood, in air, in everything—a place
that's entered you and waits for you like grace.

2.

The body learns from everything. So balance
is a brick that's held and hauled up steps
at five, and grace the holding of your baby sister
in your arms at ten. Intuition—backyard poker
games at fifteen. Even accidents, pure chance,
wet dreams and broken arms. Your youngest brother
dropping to his knees at forty, hands to chest.
This body can betray—the game can teach you
that, but also how each separate muscle flows
and how to make each movement fit together
as part of something seamless. And the rest, accept,
the way one hand at full extension must let go—
the bat beginning to fall as you are left behind,
surprised and soaring, young and wise and blind.

Phys-Ed

No one taught me what to do. I closed my fist and eyes and reached back, flailing, pulling down the curtain of the grey New England sky upon us all.

Spitting rain, early spring, gym class on the Junior high-school football field slick with guano from the flocks of gulls that flew from garbage piles across the road. And it was strange. Not that John Koval had chosen me again, for no reason at all. The way a child might cut a worm to pieces, pour salt on a slug or pull the legs from an insect. I remember the sound of his laughter like a heavy cough. Alan's, too, that same wild giggle I had heard before he pushed me down a flight of concrete steps in middle school. He didn't even try to slip away. Just stood there in the echoes.

We were running an obstacle course and John kept trying to sweep my legs, push me over, or cut me off. I was chubby, plagued with zits, but I had good balance and was quick when scared. And I *was* scared, but it was also weirdly fun. Like the thrill of driving too fast on a dirt road in the dark. John was slow, too big for his body, and I hopped and cut, leaped and scurried to the finish, first in the class, just a little winded and surprised.

When all the other kids began to disappear into the large green doors, John and Alan blocked the way. Mr. Holt, the ex-Marine Phys-Ed instructor, gave the four of us a long look, sighed, and shook his head. I still remember that: the flash of his blue tracksuit disappearing into darkness. The click of a door coming closed. The finality of death, my death. And I was alone. Except for Eric, little Eric Ross, trudging towards us, terrified, his hands pushed deep into the pockets of an oversized blue sweatshirt, taking his place like a second in a duel—stopping two feet behind me, saying nothing. John sized me up, gave a push on my shoulder. Pushed again. Looked over at Alan. Smiled brightly. Happy.

This isn't an after-school special.

I got lucky. I was terrified, and it was more a spasm than a punch. But then the crack of cartilage. And through Koval's trembling hands, so much blood.

And when I start to think that we are driven more by fear and anger, more the product of our terrors than our love, I think of Eric's arm around my back. *Holy Shit Joel, what was that, what the hell was that?* And I wept. We wept. Then laughed. Then wept. *We're fucked*, he said. *I know*, I said. *I'm fucked*, I said, *I'm fucked.*

Improvisation for Guitar

Lake Sinclair, Georgia
—*for Cyrus*

I look down and see the murmur of my bones
like deep water, like wind. My sons play the long
slope toward the shallows of Lake Sinclair, Darius
still young enough to be surprised by everything:
a flock of geese flying low, sudden splash
of stone, the way wind can wave and warp
everything. We stare as a house made of water
and light shakes, shimmers, fades completely
to reappear, become the brief home
of Canadas, of clouds, a small jet, and of course
two small children, one thin and long as the first string
of my guitar, one thick as a hammered thump
on a box. Mine and not mine, continually
altering the rhythms. Across the lake someone begins
to play piano, "Clair de Lune," then, mid-phrase, Joplin,
and I can't tell if the little boy in the house is dancing
or simply chilled by a breeze that shifts and darkens
him; a floating shadow like a veil dropped into water
takes on water and slowly sinks. If there is a pattern
here, I can't find it. Always one beat behind
and reaching like a man who thought he could play
with the best of them but can't really, can't match
the tempo shift. Doesn't know which string to hit
for what he thought was the foundation shifts,
is polyrhythmic and the house once he entered it,
not the destination but another frameless doorway
leading out and down and in.

Spontaneous Firing

Neuropathy, the doctor says, without expression. The body
shouting out its false report incessantly. *But nothing
is really wrong. Like a fire alarm going off because
the batteries are low.* Of course no warning is really false,
just late or premature, misheard or heard wrongly. Wood
wants to burn and burns and, like a poem, a flame
can leap a long way from its origins. Its logic

is its own. Somewhere, someone feels a stabbing in his chest.
The breath stops in a crib while parents sleep. Two girls
make it halfway down the steps, their lungs full
of smoke. Everything burns. And I just feel it. A month ago,
down Chellis Road at four in the morning, a house caught fire.
It burns still, smoldering in the mind's thick peat. If I had not
been sleeping, I might have seen from my bedroom window

a glowing just beyond the ridge—or maybe heard the shots
the whole town swears were there amid the pop and blast
of glass and falling beams. And maybe they were. For some
say last spring they heard the husband pointed a gun into the air

and screamed at the rain—police were called, a warning
issued, and then there were the rumors: a troubled
marriage, debt. So when the papers called it "accident,"
cause of death "asphyxia," no one believed. They heard

what they heard. *And that man was crazy,* a good friend
says. *Anyone could have seen it.* Even the minister
shakes his head. *There has to be a reason.* I nod. I know
more than I'm saying. Yes, they're always there—the signs.
Like that numbness in your left arm. Is it a pinched nerve
like you tell yourself? Or maybe heartburn. Maybe a burning
more distinct. Is it bad wiring in the walls or in the chest?
From where and when will the flames leap, the muzzle flash?
Our knowledge works only in reverse. Like a poem, like
prophecy. The fire has a logic—and, like the body, wants to burn.

Making Contact

The art of losing isn't hard to master
—Elizabeth Bishop

But sometimes losses pile up. The colder
air comes on, and contact means a sting
that burns and rises to ache in the shoulders
so the ball seems always earthbound, dying,
bone-heavy, stone-slick. Near the end
of the bench, he waits, feeling distant, older,
a nagging pain in his hips, his knees.
Years ago, in the grass lot, in mud, his sister
spent the early spring teaching him the ways
of loss—elbow up, chin to chest, wait, release.
On the back porch of the duplex, an old man
watched the failures gather and redeem—each day
a loss made elegant in young, singing veins.
Children, near, too near, and swinging at the rain.

My Son, 5, Dancing

Out of empty bags and wrapping paper,
out of the split smile of the overripe
and dripping, out of quickness of lizards
and the long-legged walk of the heron
through fog. Out of hawk-flight, out
of dawn and into the shock of the cold
pond on the groin, and the lightning-
struck tree still thrumming and warm.

Once, on the long drive home from work,
I watched an old man dance on the edge
of a bridge above the highway like
some God-stunned snake-charmer,
chin lifted, eyes raised, and lost beyond
all fearful calls beside and below—

the held breath of the world caught
on a wobbly pirouette, a heel raised

over absence. There is so much you see
and don't when you spin like a torn leaf
—when you wish to step up into wind
and be lost above rooftops.

Surfaces reflect, refract and seem
to give. Until the window
fractures. And bone. But my son,

turning and flapping the silk-
sail of the body flung
from great heights, will not settle

will not come down until the wind
in his lungs blows singing out
of blood of breath of rhythm of now

and to hell with his old man anyhow.

How to Throw the Knuckleball

Trick is, you don't use your knuckles at all,
just your fingertips. And you don't throw
it. You hang on—just long enough and then
push, guide—trust in gravity, spheres of light
on summer tar, sunspots, an old man's
drunken shuffle, a fat boy's dance

still crafty in its awkwardness. Skill and chance
and maybe a memory—some girl you know
you loved at just sixteen, her tumbling glance.
Start with that. And then, the first night
holding her—or when, weeks past the stroke,
you watched your sister learn to walk again

so beautiful you almost broke to mist right there
—that fumbled light, this ball danced into air.

Boy on the Dock

So many hulls push out
on the water, then return, leaving only
the lightest touch of the possible—of what
we dream is there. The young boy watching
from the dock travels with them as far
as he can, waits for their return, as gulls
dive, steal food from the hands of screaming
customers and fly off. Tourists putter in, debark,
talk about the day's plan, argue, settle in
and putter off again in cars too beautiful to be
real. His eyes following taillights
toward the highway, he imagines, he invents
and wonders if they saw him looking, if
the woman in the white shirt and the large
sunglasses holds him in her minds eye,
wonders what he's looking at and whose
he is. What parents. What home.

There are too many
to hold with any kind of care. It's a wonder
the boats don't sink and the cars (most of them)
make it up the hills and home with so much
to carry, so many weighted stares—each
day's haul beyond the net's capacity, beyond
the muscle it takes to pull it up and in.

Losing Names

The day I watched my father's father lose
the names of his children, some
nurse had left the TV on and the window
open. It had been days and rain
had soaked his blankets. *Dad,
it's me,* my father said, *it's Joel.* Inside
the frame someone stumbled
off the curb, arm raised
for an instant as if to hail a car,
but then a wavering, a thought
unthought as all words must unsay
themselves. When at last we all go
silent, open-mouthed, and when that silence
grows and groans with its own blossoming
like branches in a spring snowstorm, who
will wait and listen, watch us suffer,
beautiful, for what we've tried to say?

Coach

He knows, as every player knows, the game
is not life but an extension from it—his father's hands
folding over his on the ball becoming the same
hands years later, with his son. From the stands,
from the porch, in the car—late summer evenings,
the buzz of mosquitoes lingers in the night. The radio,
the television, field-lights becoming bright windows,
a child looks through to see himself reaching
through years like the outstretched arm of DiMaggio
for a lined shot, just beyond his reach. And still reaching
like Conigliaro in his prime at full extension, the ball
swerving away, always and endlessly, and yet possible
in this life, this wanting to be more than who we are
for the time that we have—this game reaching on forever.

Mud Season

The thing about remembering is that you don't forget
—Tim O'Brien

Vermont. Ripton. It comes when the ground gives way
from six tight months of frost—red clay, soil, dung softened
with the moan of aspens and the oak relaxing into April
as a hard man's fist unclenches from a ten-pound maul.
At evening. With darkness. And you can't keep it out.
Creeping into boot leather, canvas, jeans, your skin. Following
you home, across the fields, into your house, floorboards,
bedsheets, years of dreams. Where people have lost things—
whole fields of boots pulled down and smothered, chain saws,
wheelbarrows left out, sunk, taking root. Once
behind the old barn, down the sloping pasture where
the east field meets the spring, I watched a team of men
struggling to pull a horse from the earth. His forelegs lost
to the kneecaps, his chest down and forward as if
he were bending to drink or caught in descent, leaping
a fence—a moment's grace where time doesn't seem
to move or matter—but there was no grace in this. He fought,
or tried to fight, pulling against his own weight which only
made each leg sink deeper. I remember the whites of his teeth
and eyes, bared clear, whiter with fear and muck. I remember
the sound of screaming, throaty, desperate—the ropes tightening
around his waist, his legs, and the men pulling, digging, cursing
the mud, the horse, the rain, themselves and sinking still. And I
remember thinking they were all part of the same beast, brown
and heaving from the earth as if a great oak were trying to uproot
itself from the banks and walk. It was dark and raining. I was
cold and colder for being young and younger for being hopeful.

Don't ask me how this story ends. You know. And even now
the telling feels like a sinking in. Miles away, years gone, and still

when I hear the loud crack of branches in a March storm I feel it
in my chest, a breaking in the breath hitting full force, a gunshot
hovering somewhere in the tree limbs. And I know that I
won't sleep or, worse, will—having given in to the night,
to exhaustion, like some great heaving animal, his legs broken,
closing his eyes at last, sinking into the earth.

A House on the Cliff

At night the ocean shook the cottage
like an angry man will shake the shoulders
of a boy, shouting *Listen! Listen to me.* I've heard
it fill me like a sail, the way a prophet hears
God: its harsh refusal to be shut out;
a force to be lived with, not withstood.

There was a house on the cliffside.
They fought to save it. First with tires
filled with stone, poured concrete. Then shovels.
Backhoes. Cables at every joist. But one winter
storm spooned out the sand beneath. It slid
in stages, the deck leaning down the dune
like a bather stretching out one long leg to test

the water. Then the acrobatic pause—the kite
when the string snaps or stunned silence
in the stare of the child just stepping off
the curb as the car appears around
the corner. The *no, not yet* clinging on,
the diving down and in. I've heard the moan
and shriek of nails, crack of wood and glass-shatter.

Still, among the stones and driftwood,
sea-glass, bones of fish, the remnants whisper
in the sand. Broken picture frames,
a clock with the face gone—a jewelry box of silt.

BP

When all the other children had gone home,
we walked into the damp, hard consonants
of cold spring rain. The gulls and crow
crying through the pines, the crack of damp wood
in my hands—you in flannels pushed up from
your wrists and thick forearms, me in good
slacks, new cleats. Towering sixty feet away,
you were huge to me then—and distant—
calling out directions I couldn't hope to meet:
elbow up, top hand through, relax, head down.
I couldn't make it out. The ball thrown
high and tight or floating off, impossible to hit.
What could I know of contact then? Old man,
warm up your arm. Fire one in here again.

Psalms for the Fallen World

Psalms of Lamentation

1.

For when we come we must come
alone. Not with crowds or joyful
laughter or with the taste
of a lover on our lips, no. We will come
like this: 2:30 a.m., damp with sleep
and fever, children emerging from
the night terrors, blinking and
shivering, still trying to remember
and forget, inarticulate. Waiting.

2.

And yet we will come together, unaware,
staring at our own hands, amazed at their size,
thinking they are wings. We come
eyes down, palms up, speaking to ourselves
in low tones. Shoulder to shoulder on the same
narrow road, cars parked on the curbs. We
will come out of the boxes we have built
to protect ourselves from cold and rain, each
other, you. And Lord, it will have been
a long time since we have done
anything but wail our sorrow and our need.
And yet we will come muttering in combinations
without structure or form or even sense
that we could ever know. Syncopated. Already
the sirens wail in the western parts of town
and they will cry all night. Already
the bedclothes are thrown back. We come.
We lift our chins and, open-throated, sing.

3.

This is the foot slipped on the stair as we lift out
and up into the caught breath—all air. Embodied

and bodiless for a moment, hesitant, we are
and could be anywhere and anything that soars toward
impact: globe of rain, thrown stone, some satellite aflame
upon reentry—the young girl leaps from branch to porch
to slanted roof as if from lover to lover as pleading voices
call, *Careful...please come down*—thick with fear
and wonder. And there was the man in church, dropped
to his knees, glistening with heat that comes
of transmutation. We hardly breathe; we fall and we
enjoy the falling and the fallen caught mid-spiral—
the prostitutes of Degas frozen in the artist's gaze,
dancing and leaping toward a semblance of grace.

4.

This is the train-roar in the inner ear as the head comes
down, the ceiling falls away and seems to disappear.
Giving way like men and women rocking in their throws—
fuck love, forget the mortgage, fuck the furnace clanking
in the dark and the cold that always wants in through
windows and under doors. Forget the children who might
hear, above or below, in dreams confused and damp,
of other boys and girls digging in the soft flesh of the back
and flanks—the thing itself, the act, and *Oh God not yet don't
stop*. Don't worry. I won't. For this—

5.

This is what keeps on, comes on because it always comes
when we don't want it—a letter to a lover tucked in a pocket
for years, bad wiring in the walls, the bump on the head
that bursts and waits, cancer cells, the phone calls we've put
off, the debts unpaid—*what we've done and left undone*
waiting and hurtling towards us, out of us—a body thrown
through a windshield on a darkly lit road...

Or is it just there all along? Not after or before or in-
between but everywhere: Trouble. Wolves at the door.
What we hear on the outer edges of our whispering:
That impact is real and falling our condition.

6.

This is the struggle to the knees and rise. This,
our shaking as we shake our limbs to check
what works, what we can mend and can't. This,
that space we travel and become that is
still instant and insistent and is ours.

7.

Lord, I have wanted to ask you
where you are, but I know
it is the wrong question. Even
if you'd answer, it wouldn't keep
the pipes from bursting or clean
the air, stop the swine flu or
the bird flu. Yesterday a girl
in my son's class stepped out into
the road and was run down. She
was on the crosswalk. She obeyed
the light, the guard. She was
a good girl. They found her
tennis shoe across the street
in the parking lot of
the Baskin-Robbins.

8.

We wait and wait. We freeze and sweat
and freeze again, shivering in frosted sheets,
and nothing and no one comes that wasn't always
arriving and leaving all along—boxcars,
interchangeable as days, as years, shuddering

the ground enough to let us feel their passing rise
up through the platform to our calves and thighs,
to tremble for an instant in the pelvis, in the ribcage.

Necks aching with the strain

of prayer, the thought that this is all that matters—
beyond the boxes and the basements we have built
along the railroads and the ports and highways
promising transcendence, change, ascension—this
careening stillness, this midnight desperate
groping after body heat that leaves us

flickering.

9.

Asked for songs of praise, what do we return
but broken things—romanticized, ugly, violent
or prim. This jagged metonymy. A finger
represents a hand, stands for a girl; the bedpost
the bed, its shaking for a shaken world. Even
pleasure twisted like thread pulled idly from
the silk. We've come undone, pieced ourselves
apart and served that up, said *here, you can have
this much* or *I'll take that and leave the rest*
when all along the streets one could
and should feel, at any time of day or night, in
back rooms and in basements and kitchens,
on every surface that will hold our weight, the shiver
of whole bodies pressed in flight, hands fluttering
up across the bones of the back, mouths half-open,
eyes rolled back so that all roads and paths,
interstates and sidewalks are like taut
strings plucked by the same plectrum.

The Noise We Make

We have to learn again to listen
the way as children we once
learned to see in glimpses through
legs of men, through cornrows, through
the cracks of light in doorways
and sun-blind classroom windows,
listen around corridors, through echo
and the engine's thrum—the shush and push
of everything that moves and keeps
on moving through the noise we make
to rise above the noise—and stop
our breathing in our throats, our beating
blood, reaching to the place where silence
doesn't have to mean that we're alone,
only that we're listening together.

Stones

In the clutch of a child, each stone is a prayer,
a night-slung shadow thrown from the arm's whip
through windows of abandoned homes, off
the hot flat roofs of tenements, down sewers, and out
into the darkness of oceans and of woods. The stone,
a thought flung far beyond the limits of the body
that cannot fly or fall too far without echo.

Body Memory

Once, a boy, out walking the access road along
Route 1, I watched a woman jump (or was she
pushed) from the bed of a truck, her body spun into
fields of tall grass and gravel. And when she rose,
holding her head in her hands, bleeding, standing,
she came up slow, in pain. Unfolding. Every inch
alight in pain. Mouth wide, silent. And the truck
pulling away, the door still open, swinging wild
as it made the corner onto the highway.

Still I am shocked, not by how fragile
we are, but how easily transformed. Did she
will her self to stand, some signal shouting, *Up,
damn-it. Up!* or did she simply find herself
upright again, still stunned to have fallen, to be
this person in this moment, a strange boy
staring at her? I watched for a moment,
thought *My God,* and took off running. Dust

on my tongue—terrified and young and trying
to outdistance the image of one who rose
from the ground, from the surely dead, who swayed
and shook, then, sunstruck, dropped to earth again.

The Well

Beyond the field behind my house I found
an abandoned well covered in old planks,
a blanket of moss, and pine mulch. I could not
see to water but inhaled the rot and wet
and thought it might go down forever, curve
into a belly like the long plumed throat of a loon.
Stone after stone I dropped into the earth
and listened. No splash, no thud, no clack and clatter.
There, amid the pines and calls of birds,
there was only the swallowing of stones
and the low, long breathing of a boy.

South Side Aneurysm—6:10 A.M.

I feel it, rising, flooding beneath our feet, shifting from stones hove
up with heat and cold where, years ago, rough hands tore the earth to lay
the veins of the town, tearing out gravel, the roots of trees, pipe laid by
other men who lost their farms before the war—who joked in German,
French, Czech, broken tongues above a broken earth. I hear them in the
whine that resonates in old metal bursting with hard work and fifty years,
bearing water from the reservoir, from the river, home to home, to haul
away our filth into septic tanks or back into the rivers where it disappears
(or is it always moving among us, out of sight, in the dark) like secrets
hidden in closets, like love poems written to the wrong man or woman,
like an unpaid bill, like the men five miles south in the state penitentiary
who bend in the halls and drink this same fluoridated, calcified, purified,
iron-rich and state-approved water rising up through the basement of
every home, connecting us all in one smooth, reliable current, borne by
bucket on the head of a villager or up from the well by strong arms or into
the veins of a child, heated by the growing of her body to become, years
later, the vein in the back of the mind, sequenced in the DNA to explode
somewhere in the vast network of pipes at exactly 6:15 in the morning as
the ground cools and barometric pressure rises, then suddenly falls, and the
metal groans one last time. At the exact moment when the old woman
who lives on the corner pulls the chain on an antique toilet, the main will
burst like everything that lives and flows and is confined in the rich current
of the world and, like water, must come rising from beneath us, soaking
the earth, chasing the possum from the sewer, the cat from the shelter
beneath the house, flooding the street as it shifts and roars, become a river,
become the artery of the town made visible and boiling with first light, lost
languages, hidden notes, the roar of the man in the cell, the roar of the
woman as she falls, her brain swelling, her arm going numb, the roar of
the child who laughs at it all from her window, the roar of water and the
carrying of water that knows no language but is always sending and
receiving a message we cannot know or live without, here in the pipe
that is always bursting.

Storage

I can't seem to get away from them. Boxes [in the basement. Boxes in the backs of closets. Boxes shoved beneath the beds. Things] I can't unstack [unpack]. I pop the trunk of my Corolla and a box of books gapes back— one cardboard flap, flap flapping [with the memory of words I've read and left unread] [the motion of their movement like lips whispering] in silence [long after the choir has stopped]. The wedding photos [of the widower] must go [somewhere, piled up in storage] with ten years of tax returns, ten years of birthday cards. One box full of finger paintings [suns and seas and smudgy greens of mountains, grassy fields] where all the families skip hand in hand among the wildflowers, smiling [and intact]. For years I've tried to bury them [by unburying, slicing packing tape along the seams, staring in, selecting, unselecting, then, taping up the box again]. Each [unburdening a] burden, each [opening a] wound, [a surgery] that left behind an ache [that thumps and rattles on its way to whatever space I've made to hide it in] until the closets wouldn't close, the ceiling bowed beneath the weight. This weekend [this month, this year] we'll [get to the storage room, the attic] clean it out, I tell myself. [But don't. And hope my back grows strong, and legs.] Shore up the beams and girders. Find a bigger house in yet another town where I can store everything I could not save [and failed to throw away].

Fire

On the burning of a small theatre in Omaha, Nebraska

Like most, I have been more the watcher of fires
than the fire itself or even the arsonist or the one who falls
        asleep in the attic studio with the space heater running. I
remember, as a child, loving the smolder and smoke
        of leaf-piles burning along the roadside long before
we knew that smoke could kill us, and later the slow

        glow of the cigarette, and now the hearth, the logs' creak
and murmur, the hiss of sap, water bursting in the veins,
        the warm skin on the cheek. And I have named
the world for it—blood's rise, wild clematis flaming out
        of late November, a strange dawn of snow in freezing rain,

the failed painter in the studio who will never be more
        than she is at the moment; the palette knife edges the canvas
and the canvas itself gives to her, becomes knife, arm
        that holds it, a voice in the hall below practicing some

monologue to no one and so is merely voice, streetcar, echo
        of a spark that is not a thing, really, but pure result, a catching
and climbing itself in air, into the next element, the next
        possibility of burning until it is exhausted, gone,

something lost in the eyes of an audience,
        smoke rising blooming from streetlamps, then sirens,
with old wood cracking under its own exhalation and plaster
        bubbling from walls and gunshot report of the stone step

that splits with heat. The young woman worrying for her apartment.
        The frightened child who clings to her, still fervid with dreams.

And the policeman who called it in, thinking *Thank God.*

        No one was inside. No one lived here. The zip of oils

catching fire in the dark.

The Contortionists

Parentheses are jarring to the reader. The temptation to use parentheses is a clue that a sentence is becoming contorted
—APA Style manual

Everything (that matters) happens (in parenthesis) on the margins (in the alleyways and basements) where something waits (and broods) its many voices grope (like virgins in the dark) echoing themselves in moans for all that we have pushed away (or lock inside the way the acrobat will bend and fold each bone and muscle of each limb into a small glass box before her slim wrist rises and the long pale fingers flip the lid down after her to click it shut so one strong man can swing her by the handle to the gasping of a titillated crowd) (only to unfurl herself again as if the body were no more a thing of bone and cartilage than silk drawn out by hands in acts of conjuring) all peoples need their revolutionaries (all cities need the ones who won't stay on the sidewalks or sit quiet on the bus but) (need that first bluesman who thought to sit there on the stoop and bend a string then thought again to drag a bottleneck along a note to make it cry and sing and need that song the way the worshipers in pews or on their knees or counting beads besides their beds all need their heretics) the ones who make things (break things) new like dervishes who spin until the universe (begins to warp and bend contort into another thing and then another until each movement) is a dance and all dances (praise and all words) poetry (especially the ones we didn't say that caught within our chests and throats) like sobs like laughter waiting to (re)make the world (im)possible (again).

Communion

At the grocery store, post office, public restrooms, we
take up as little space as possible, we pull ourselves
into ourselves, look away, stare longingly,
close our eyes, slide down into our seats, slip through
and into pockets. Illicit shameful things, we
move together but apart, mumbling to ourselves
our absolutions, and sidle away unnervingly. And all along
Route 60, caught in traffic, caught in lines, we move
like long notes wavering distinct above the melody.
In and out of pitch and almost

out of time at five p.m. in JB's Gentleman's Club, bodies
supplicate and wait for even the lightest touch.
You understand the rules? the dancer asks.
The man nods, hands twitching at his sides.
At Gina's Lounge, someone pulls the lever
on the slot down and down and down
until his eyes begin to water. The chat rooms are all
full tonight. The frequency of witness that is
not witness. The hum that is the chorus of who
would speak for us. Who at last will say, will sing

this psalm of silences. Cesaurae. Desperate, the out-
of-work nail technician throws open the door
of her Camry in the middle of the intersection where
her timing belt has snapped like a piano string,
like a wire deep within her chest. She shouts into her
cell. A chain grinds around an axle. A weight
lifts. An engine starts. A man says *I am so
tired so hungry* and the street says *yes.*
A woman says *I am so cold* and the night says *yes
yes.* The chassis rocks beneath us, the wind shakes
all the wires high above the boulevard, a chin lifts
up as if in prayer, and the lips say *yes.*

What to Say

In the long moment after love with her arm under your arm, her fingers at your chest, her hips moving a little behind you, your bodies still warm and flushed when she says *Lover?* and you murmur *yes* and she says *How did you learn to touch a woman?* First, lie there a moment, take your time, thank whatever God you worship, but take care of how you answer. Don't puff out your chest and lower your voice like Elvis. Don't say *Trial and error baby.* Don't tell her about that older woman at the bar when you were twenty who took your hand beneath her blue velvet skirt. Don't talk of some book you read as a boy. And never, never bring up porn—if you are man who likes porn, which means you probably haven't been asked this question anyway. No, tell her where all touchings start: on the edge of a beach as child, the burning sand in your toes, salt on your tongue, shorts clinging, and that first feeling, first stirring of blood. Tell her how you always loved the feel of the world. Tell how, in the store with your mother, you'd push your hands into racks of clothes and feel crinoline, taffeta, cotton, corduroy, satin, silk. How your tongue would creep to your teeth and slip out and your mother and your sisters would laugh and blush. Let her laugh because she's seen you do it with her. Tell her how you'd linger in sleep and roll in that softness for hours. Tell of the summer when you were thirteen and your parents got you the paper route so you could lose that paunch at your middle, only you didn't because, slick with your own heat, you'd roll into the dairy, feel the cold blast all over you, and order a milkshake so you could feel God's own glory slip down your throat. How you grew fat and sassy. Tell her you've always, always been touching the world. Tell her how, working one summer as a landscaper, you'd go into woods without your shirt because you liked the tiny scratches, the feel of the leaves on your back. How you'd plant tulips and shrubs without gloves so you'd spend days with dirt beneath your fingernails. Tell her of that time at the bar when you were 17 and way too young and way too drunk to go home and you first really *felt* the blues through your feet and the vibration of the table and the soft touch of that voice all over you, coming from the stage, from a woman who did not move so much as roll her body to and away from you, who sang bodily, entering the microphone, entering you layer by layer. Tell her how there are days since you met her when you swear you can touch the wall of any building and feel the lovers in the corner apartment on the second floor on the west side making love. Tell her everything. Tell it all if you can because you can and she'll listen. Or, better, don't—because its not an answer she was looking for. Linger in the silence more. Say *lover,* say *love,* and touch and touch and touch.

Listen Hear

Because you can't technique your way to grace any more than lovers locked
in sweat could or would prefer the precision of a calculating touch, *Listen.*
I have read the long road to the Temple Mount was desolate. That there
were lions in the desert. And bandits. And yet that, on high holidays, whole
villages would dance and stumble, ride and sing their way through heat
and cold and trouble, the youngest and the eldest clinging to each other on
the backs of donkeys or carried or dragged by strong hands. How they
camped along the road, stirring their pots amid the wheeling silence of the
stars, no protection but each other, the road their guide, the object—
something that they'd never see but hoped to know—rising up like embers
in the dark, up temple steps likes psalms. Last night Rachael, driving home
from work, passed a body in the street covered in white. Blue lights slid
along the panels of slow-moving cars. *There were policemen, waiving us
along,* she said. *You couldn't help but look. It was a body. In the road.* On the
news, they say she stepped off of the curb and the woman heading home
from choir practice hit her going forty. Flush. Now the road is clear, and
Rachael waves a hand toward the McDonald's drive-thru by the Cancer
Center. *Here. It happened here, I think.* Because, just for a moment,
everything slowed and came together, pooled and shimmered, brightening
with headlights and wonder. Because you can't just sit there, can't just stare
on blankly at the screen. You have to listen, pay attention. Think of Charlie
Parker, thirteen hours into practicing and slicing clean each note, perfect,
on a brand-new horn, each breath hurting from the ribs he'd cracked when
a touring car slipped off the road out in the Ozarks into darkness. And
trees and snow and stars had spun. And some of them were thrown and
some were crushed and he was left on the cold road, broken but alive,
alone. How he began to hear the many voices chattering in different
rooms, the buzz of ball games on the radio, the news, dishes clattering, the
heavy sigh of busses, metal-on-metal scraping garbage cans upended into
trucks, each a player—some quick-fingered, others lingering on tones and
hues deep-dyed in red, and others, earth-toned greens, and browns, and
blues—entering the song, knocking him off balance until he thought to let
them in, speak back and through, to imitate, rephrase and listen to the
way each rhythm made it new; that, to see or feel a pattern, a progression,
like a body, must be broken—just a little and a little more—so broken

patterns pile up like fifty heartbeats in a field of crickets or the springs of every mattress, every bedpost bumping on a wall, each baby's wail in each apartment breaking it, reshaping it into some semblance of a song that all the careful work and practicing will only teach you how to replicate, not make, invent. Because it's there in front of you like warm skin yielding to your touch, the catch of breath that tells you *yes* or *yes, but gentler, there* and *please* and opens like a body, blooms like blood rising into beaded sweat to shine and slip, to glimmer in the lamplight, moonlight, streetlight, headlights gliding into rivulets to run down trembling, pooling in the hollow of the abdomen. Because like thieves, like lions, trouble comes, it always comes, or is it waiting just outside the door, listening—or not waiting, really, but just there, past the next hill or hurtling at, not toward, you and surprised as you by you to find you on that road, stepping off that curb; and you must know that terror, too, and hunger that would lead us to this place, this moment when the wide eyes lock with knowing that it's happening right now, right here, and there is no time left to step back up to safety, halt the impact and the aftermath. Because this morning, stirring coffee while you watched the news of how a woman was run down on Hal Greer Boulevard as she tried to cross the street to see her husband in the hospital, and the ones who witnessed and who came to help saying *It's just a shame she had to lose her life like that,* I thought of how the woman in the SUV weaving in an out of cars must have felt so good, so comforted, to have sung each note so that it fit exactly with the others—perfect harmony, almost as good as the record. Because I have been there too, my back cooling on the pavement, pelvis shattered, staring up out of the wreckage of my life, my wife crushed in the car, my oldest son thrown fifty feet beyond, already gone as far as any star that burned itself to cinders in another galaxy a hundred thousand years ago. Because of what we see and do not see up there and how I want to step back up and out and listen, see how all of it or some of it at least can be more than accidental notes a child hammers on the keys or, better, find a way to shape those sounds into a song, a psalm that breaks apart and comes together with yours, whoever you are, whatever key you're playing in, and let it be as fresh as first love, first light, to hold and keep each candle flame alight, each cooking fire, each star within it burning, trembling, just beneath your skin. It's no wonder Charlie Parker died from heroin.

Gospel

We shall gather at the river, yes, but also
at terminals and depots. We will stand,
hands raised, dodging the sleet-spray
of taxis. Asleep on benches and up
against the soot-gray walls
of Greyhound stations from Nashville
to Flint. In packs, jostling
for the window seat, rolling
our eyes and sighing.
And we will carry everything we are
in bags *no taller than 22 inches, no wider
than 14, no deeper than 9.* We will come
together hurtling at killing speed,
surrounded by unbreathable air and bitter
cold sunlight so bright it burns the corneas.
We will read our books and sleep,
gathered and dispersed; then, regrouped
at baggage claims and rental counters,
long-term parking on the margins
of the highways that would appear
as shining silver rivers, if only
they were clear of each and every
fitful one of us, traveling alone.

Sermon

1.

And the people will gather. Having
Come to the Sermon At The Mountaintop
Removal—also called The Sermon By
The Concentrated Animal Feeding Operation
or in some texts referenced equally as
The Sermon At The Elevated Parking
Garage or The Sermon at the Walmart
or the Sermon Where The Plain Used
To Be but no one will remember where
or what a "plain" was and so will finally
and more accurately be called The Sermon
Over There Where All Those People
Are Gathering...

2.

This blasting rocks the earth, tears
it at the coal seams. World become
Energy. Peak performance. Yield.
It takes people who can see a tree only
for how long it takes to burn to rip the sky
itself apart. Toxins seep into the rivers
and run off down the mountainside with deer
or float as ash into bird-wheeling absences
of dusk and shadow. And we are long past
no please don't and *stop.* Somewhere past
exhaustion (when all the soil, stone, and roots
settle into overburden dumped into a holler-
fill or shaped again to form the approximate
contours of the mountains, only softer,
throbbing like a bruise) people will return—
perhaps a man sloshing through a river
with a boy. They speak in low tones, listening
for once and before and maybe, new grass
growing on a hill where the valley used to be.

Psalm 23

Eighteen-wheelers lean close as they pass
or stalk the rearview, hovering above the shadow
of my son—long rocked to sleep in the hollow
of this dark palm, this gorge we travel through
on 68. The semis reel me back, grow massive—chrome,
steel, and predatory—with the whine of gravity,
a very great weight pressing twenty tons

to our backs like rough hands, like shame—
half-buried things—how we find the ways to hurt
ourselves, each other. I have been the boot
that blows the door from the hinges, from the frames.
I've been the hands held up against the rain
of blows. I've been the caller and the called
and, like a hungry owl, followed the cry
to its source in the throat and the chest
of the child waking to a world he cannot see
beyond the light that freezes, shatters, breaks
apart and whirls in crystals as they sweep
and dance like galaxies blown across the tops

of trailers. And now I've been this man
who says *Sleep, child, sleep. It is well, and when*
you wake we will be home, my voice
become sure as any god who could ball
the whirling stars up with the snow and the night
itself, reach back and throw it far beyond
the firmament and over the tops of mountains

and the caught breath of wolves
and the woman who works the night shift
at the BP high up on the mountain, trying
to decide if she should brave the drive
or wait it out till morning. I have been this voice

that says *I know* and knows we can't know
anything—but listens, trying to resist the urge
to let it go, shifting into higher gears that will not
hold us back but send us lurching into fall and let
the taut jaw slacken with release and slip
and spin. I've been this man afraid and rolling

toward home, my son in the back seat absent
as the dead and just as present—in the way love's
tethers rope us to this earth, ourselves,
the night—my fingers gripped around its wheel.

God's Bicycle

God is peddling a bicycle down
Highway 32, traveling west toward
Cincinnati against traffic (of course).
The bicycle is red—one of the sit-down,
layback types with three wheels and
a basket on the front filled with groceries:
local eggs, milk, cheese, some bacon.
(He hasn't been Kosher in years.) A Bengals
pennant blows from the back. (Who
knew?!) He looks much like you'd expect
—a fat, elderly white guy with a soot-stained
beard and the slightly crazed and haggard look

of the father of many (many) children when
the children figure out he loves them
and that, really, there is little he can do—
a time-out here, a spanking there.
Even if the burning pit is real, he will not
drop them. So they fight and bicker,
pull at his ears, laugh at shouts and idle
threats, beat the dog, masturbate on
the toilet, in the closet, in the basement,
on his favorite couch when he's at work

and leave the stains for him to clean.
Saying *I know what you've been up to,*
I'm everywhere does nothing (since
the Puritans) but make them exhibitionists
or hypocrites—at best voyeurs. And what
did all that watching do to him at last
but make his eyes sore? So he leans back
in his pajama pants and flannels, peddling
his bicycle, his chin raised skyward so

he can't see into the windows, can't
meet the hungry stares. And it is
a miracle how he avoids collisions

(mostly) and keeps the world in orbit.
There is enough to do—*Get out
of the way you crazy old*—switching
gears from high to low, muttering,
as he goes, *I love you all I love
you I love you I love you all I
love you.*

Acknowledgments

Grateful acknowledgment is made to the following publications in which some of these poems originally appeared.

580-Split: "Communion"

A Ritual to Read Together: Poems in Conversation with William Stafford (Longman): "The Noise We Make"

Academic Questions: "Psalms of Lamentation 1 and 2"

Aethlon: "Making Contact," "Infield/Outfield"

American Society: What Poets See (FutureCycle Press): "Sermon I," "Sermon II"

The Ampersand Review: "Everything Must Go"

And Love (Jacar Press): "You Tell Me All My Love Poems Are About Myself"

Beloit Poetry Journal: "The Well"

The Black Warrior Review: "O Street"

The Boiler: "Husks I," "Husks II"

Borderlands: Texas Poetry Review: "Traffic"

The Connecticut Review: "U-Haul"

The Connecticut River Review: "Psalm 96," "Peace and the Valley," "Losing Names"

Contemporary Poetry of New England (University Press of New England): "Mud Season"

The Dos Passos Review: "The Basement Man"

Elysian Fields: "BP"

The Edge: "God's Bicycle"

Jelly Bucket: "Psalms of Lamentation 1-8"

Many Mountains Moving: "Fire"

theNewerYork: "Listen Hear"

Passages North: "South Side Aneurysm"

Prairie Schooner: "The House on the Cliff," "Spontaneous Firing," "Living in Layers"

Rattle: "Body Memory"

Slab: "The Contortionists"

The Southern Review: "Improvisation for Guitar," "Movers and Shakers," "In the Next Seat"

Spillway: "Stones," "Psalm 23"

Sport Literate: "The Coach"
Storm Cellar: "Phys-Ed"
The Valparaiso Poetry Review: "My Son, 5, Dancing," "Blind Spots"

"Boy on the Dock" and "Everything Must Go" were originally published in the chapbook, *Movers and Shakers* (Pudding House, 2010).

"Fire" and "What to Say" were originally published in *The Heat of What Comes* (Pecan Grove Press).

Cover artwork, "to work by bike," by vannmarie; author photo by Rachael Peckham; cover and interior book design by Diane Kistner; Minion Pro text and Benguiat Gothic titling

About FutureCycle Press

FutureCycle Press is dedicated to publishing lasting English-language poetry books, chapbooks, and anthologies in both print-on-demand and ebook formats. Founded in 2007 by long-time independent editor/publishers and partners Diane Kistner and Robert S. King, the press incorporated as a nonprofit in 2012. A number of our editors are distinguished poets and writers in their own right, and we have been actively involved in the small press movement going back to the early seventies.

The FutureCycle Poetry Book Prize and honorarium is awarded annually for the best full-length volume of poetry we publish in a calendar year. Introduced in 2013, our Good Works projects are anthologies devoted to issues of universal significance, with all proceeds donated to a related worthy cause. Our Selected Poems series highlights contemporary poets with a substantial body of work to their credit; with this series we strive to resurrect work that has had limited distribution and is now out of print.

We are dedicated to giving all of the authors we publish the care their work deserves, making our catalog of titles the most diverse and distinguished it can be, and paying forward any earnings to fund more great books.

We've learned a few things about independent publishing over the years. We've also evolved a unique, resilient publishing model that allows us to focus mainly on vetting and preserving for posterity the most books of exceptional quality without becoming overwhelmed with bookkeeping and mailing, fundraising activities, or taxing editorial and production "bubbles." To find out more about what we are doing, come see us at www.futurecycle.org.

The FutureCycle Poetry Book Prize

All full-length volumes of poetry published by FutureCycle Press in a given calendar year are considered for the annual FutureCycle Poetry Book Prize. This allows us to consider each submission on its own merits, outside of the context of a contest. Too, the judges see the finished book, which will have benefitted from the beautiful book design and strong editorial gloss we are famous for.

The book ranked the best in judging is announced as the prize-winner in the subsequent year. There is no fixed monetary award; instead, the winning poet receives an honorarium of 20% of the total net royalties from all poetry books and chapbooks the press sold online in the year the winning book was published. The winner is also accorded the honor of being on the panel of judges for the next year's competition; all judges receive copies of all contending books to keep for their personal library.

CPSIA information can be obtained at www.ICGtesting.com
Printed in the USA
LVOW04s1056040915

452444LV00020B/281/P

9 781938 853616